"Nadina has done a masterful job of turning her own life's challenges into victory through the power of the Word of God. For anyone with their own emotional challenges – or even for those who just want more of the Lord – Nadina's book will take you there."

LONNIE LANE
Restoring Ancient Paths Ministries

"upROOTED is a well scriptural balanced book on the subject of deliverance. In this book, I feel that it is saturated with revelations that many Christians are blinded to. There are spiritual forces that work behind the scenes in the lives of many people including Christians. Nadina Williams explains in her book, by way of confessions, an important aspect needed in rebuilding broken walls of the spirit, so we don't have to be living with strongholds. I strongly recommend this book be read by everyone, and to be used as a study material by Teachers and Bible Colleges."

ELAINE GRANT
Executive VP Women's Ministry
Intercessor, Pastoral Care

"… In presenting God's words, Nadina lucidly shows God's goodness from her viewpoint, as well as some self-searching exercises. Her approach in bringing Christ's goodness gives readers a new outlook on life's struggles. To all those who are seeking a clearer understanding of Christ's dealing with lost humanity, I am convinced that the Spirit-filled messages in this book will inspire you and result not only in personal victory over sin but also in a fresh desire and ability to share the Christian life and hope with others, despite their religious affiliation - young and old, male and female, longstanding or newly converts. I, therefore, heartily recommend a serious reading of this book."

V. A. PATRICE
Teacher

*up*ROOTED
A Manual of Deliverance

Nadina Williams

Storehouse Media Group, LLC
Jacksonville, Florida

upROOTED: A Manual of Deliverance

Copyright © 2017 by Nadina Williams

All rights reserved by author. The author guarantees all content is original and do not infringe upon the legal rights of any other person or work. No part of this publication may be reproduced, distributed, or transmitted in any form or by any means, including photocopying, recording, or other electronic or mechanical methods, without the prior written permission of the Author, except in the case of brief quotations embodied in critical reviews and certain other noncommercial uses permitted by copyright law. For permission requests, email Author at email address below and type in subject line: "Attention: Permissions Coordinator."

Storehouse Media Group, LLC
Jacksonville, Florida
www.StorehouseMediaGroup.com
publish@StorehouseMediaGroup.com

Ordering Information:
Quantity sales. Special discounts are available with the Publisher at the email address above and type in subject line "Special Sales Department."

Unless otherwise indicated, Bible quotations are taken from the Holy Bible, King James Version.

upROOTED: A Manual of Deliverance / Nadina Williams —1st ed.

ISBN: 978-1-943106-22-6 (paperback)
ISBN: 978-1-943106-23-3 (ebook)

Library of Congress Control Number: 2017963112

Printed in the United States of America

Dedication

In honor of my Heavenly Father,
who I bestow the title of
"author" of this book

Acknowledgments

All glory and honor to my Heavenly Father for the given inspiration to produce this book. For without His divine orchestration the completion of this book would not have been made possible. Heartfelt thanks to my husband, Walt Williams, for his enormous love and support in the birthing of the book. Thank you to my dear sister in Christ, Sherill Williams, for the support and belief in this printed word. I would also like to extend my gratitude to Vanessa Patrice, Elaine Grant, Lonnie Lane and Sherrie Clark for their contribution in the creation of the book. To the person reading this, special thanks also to you.

Letter from the Co-Author

My dear brothers and sisters,

I knew that I undoubtedly loved God but there were times when I would knowingly and unknowingly do or say things that were not Christ-like. Holy Spirit would convict me in those times and I would be left feeling disappointed in myself for disappointing God. I didn't know why I would behave the way I did, but I knew my behavior was hindering me from fully experiencing God. Through seeking the Lord's face, I found the root, or should I say the roots of my problem. Stored up in my heart were unresolved hurts and pains, and selfish promises to protect myself over the course of my life. The thing is I had received a new life, but I held onto the baggage of my past life. It was not because I wanted to, instead it was quite the opposite. I didn't know how to let go. I tell you this - there is nothing like having your heavenly Father take you through the process of healing and deliverance Himself. This book does just that. It gives you the opportunity to be one with God to bring you healing and deliverance.

It has always been my Father's intended purpose to have me share this with you and I say this with all pureness of heart: He is waiting on you!

Contents

Introduction..xiii

Chapter I: The Source of the Roots 1

Chapter II: A Study of the Heart 10

Chapter III: Guard Your Heart 41

Chapter IV: Strongholds 44

Chapter V: Setting Your Heart Free 48

Chapter VI: The Root of the Matter 64

Conclusion 71

About the Author: NADINA WILLIAMS 73

Introduction

"Counsel in the heart of man is like deep water;
but a man of understanding will draw it out"
(Proverbs 20:5).

Truly, God has insight into our hearts (its intents, desires, joys and sorrows), and there comes a time in our lives when God grants us the understanding to draw from it what are needed and not needed for our walk with Him. The foundation of this book started with my own deliverance and in the process God has instructed that it be shared. It is for this reason that I consider myself the co-author and the Lord the author. Luke 8:15 says ***"But that on the good ground are they, which in an honest and good heart, having heard the word, keep it, and bring forth fruit with patience."*** During our life on earth many seeds are sown in our hearts from our good and bad experiences. However, it is our Savior's desire for us to not preserve the negative seeds, such as anger, hate, and unforgiveness. Instead, He wants us after having learned the truth of His word, to retain it in our hearts so that our hearts may produce a crop that is pleasing to Him.

God does not want our hearts to be divided, nor does He want hearts of stone. Every so often our hearts become hard after experiencing many hurts and pains. However, God clearly defines His purpose in these experiences and instead removes the heart of stone. He illustrates this in Ezekiel 11:19 saying,

"And I will give them one heart, and I will put a new spirit within you; and I will take the stony heart out of their flesh, and will give them an heart of flesh." Many of the things of God that are designed to come from our hearts cannot come unless our hearts are made pure. The bible says in 1 Timothy 1:5 (NIV) that love comes from a pure heart *"The goal of this command is love, which comes from a pure heart and a good conscience and a sincere faith."* A person whose heart is filled with hate finds it difficult to love. A person whose heart is filled with evil thoughts and intents cannot serve God. Today, I encourage you and would like you to know that God desires your heart and He wants to rid your heart of any seeds that the enemy would have sown. God has made it available for us to have a new heart and I trust that after reading this book your heart will be made new.

"Cast away from you all your transgressions, whereby ye have transgressed; and make you a new heart and a new spirit: for why will ye die, O house of Israel?" (Ezekiel 18:31).

"For God, who commanded the light to shine out of darkness, hath shined in our hearts, to give the light of the knowledge of the glory of God in the face of Jesus Christ" (2 Corinthians 4:6).

CHAPTER I

The Source of the Roots

*"The thief cometh not, but for to steal, and to kill,
and to destroy: I am come that they might have life,
and that they might have it more abundantly"
(John 10:10).*

**"But the God of all grace, who hath called us unto his
eternal glory by Christ Jesus, after that ye have suffered a
while, make you perfect, stablish, strengthen, settle you"
(1 Peter 5:10)**

If you are reading this book and somehow want to put it down
or you don't have time for this and/or you suddenly feel no
desire to read, then you need to silence the voice of the
enemy, for what you are about to read, and experience is very
serious. The devil's mission is to kill, steal and destroy
everything concerning your life and even life itself, but Jesus
Christ came to give life and bring redemption and restoration.
The truth is, in life the devil will attempt to kill, steal and
destroy some things in your life. However, we have much to
be grateful for, in that we know our Heavenly Father wants
not one of us to perish. Even though the enemy would have

tampered with your life, God will use it for His glory. One way to know God's calling for your life or your ministry is to just look at the struggles that you have been faced with and have overcome and you will know. For example, if you have battled and have been delivered from being possessed or influenced by the devil it may be that your ministry is deliverance. If you have always been attacked with sickness and received healing perhaps your ministry is healing.

Remember we are His testimonies and witnesses on the earth. Be encouraged, that the Lord says, "ALL things work together for our good..." If we trust God and love Him, He will work all things out, not for our destruction but for our establishment in Him.

"And we know that all things work together for good to them that love God, to them who are the called according to his purpose" (Romans 8:28).

For many of us, the enemy starts when we are young, hoping that by the time he finishes sowing all the seeds he possibly can we will be bitter, wanting to have absolutely nothing to do with knowing or serving God. The seeds he plants are the events in our lives that result in us having or exhibiting negative attributes. The more we exhibit those negative feelings, the more they become a part of us. God will allow us to feel and experience negative feelings, but it is what we do with them or about them that matters. It is evident that negative and evil ways may become a part of us if not dealt with properly, and it is for this reason God requires that we rid ourselves from negative feelings, emotions, habits and ways. Positive thoughts create positive feelings, negative thoughts create negative feelings. The Lord's plan for us is to restore us fully unto Him.

"For I know the thoughts that I think toward you, saith the Lord, thoughts of peace, and not of evil, to give you an expected end. Then shall ye call upon me, and ye shall go and pray unto me, and I will hearken unto you. And ye shall seek me, and find me, when ye shall search for me with all your heart. And I will be found of you, saith the Lord: and I will turn away your captivity, and I will gather you from all the nations, and from all the places whither I have driven you, saith the Lord; and I will bring you again into the place whence I caused you to be carried away captive" (Jeremiah 29:11-14).

When God has a purpose for your life, He makes sure that your mind, heart and soul are in tune with Him and belongs to Him. If you belong to the Lord, you will bear His fruits and cultivate a tree that is deeply rooted in Him.

"Ye shall know them by their fruits. Do men gather grapes of thorns, or figs of thistles? Even so every good tree bringeth forth good fruit; but a corrupt tree bringeth forth evil fruit. A good tree cannot bring forth evil fruit, neither can a corrupt tree bring forth good fruit. Every tree that bringeth not forth good fruit is hewn down, and cast into the fire. Wherefore by their fruits ye shall know them" (Matthew 7: 16-20).

God's purpose and promises for our lives are hindered when we have a negative mindset, a troubled heart and soul. Having all three is evident that the tree planted within us is bad (evil). Have you ever seen a Christian who is very judgmental and seem to criticize everyone or everything? Well, this is a Christian who has a bad tree growing within him or her. Please know that this does not mean that he or she doesn't love God and does not have a desire to serve Him, but because he or she has some unresolved issues, hurts and/or pains that are causing him or her to bear bad fruits.

Many of us are just like the person in the above scenario. God's purpose and promises for my life were very much affected because of childhood trauma. I became a Christian at the age of twenty and every purpose I felt that God had for me was questioned even after several months of them being fulfilled. One of those purposes was of my marriage. The Lord said that my marriage was to be a replica of how Christian marriages should be. I had a challenging time believing this purpose because almost everything caused disagreement.

I remember always asking God what it was that I was doing wrong, until one day He answered. He shared with me that there was a tree that the enemy had planted within my heart that He wanted out. This tree was rooted in negative feelings and negative experiences, thus, producing the negative fruits that I was seeing. During my encounter with the Lord, my husband and I were in a dispute at the time. He did not know my struggle, nor what I was praying for. One day I made a drawing of the tree that was within me, under the guidance of the Holy Spirit, and showed it to my husband. I remember him getting all choked up and he said, "Do you know what the Lord told me? He told me that all of our difficulties were happening so that He could get some things out of you that

He wants out." Hearing this made me realize, more than ever, that it was time that Colossians 3:8 was made manifest in my life, which says, *"But now ye also put off all these..."* I was to now rid myself of the seeds that produced this negativity so that my life would yield good fruit.

"Another parable put he forth unto them, saying, The kingdom of heaven is likened unto a man which sowed good seed in his field: But while men slept, his enemy came and sowed tares among the wheat, and went his way. But when the blade was sprung up, and brought forth fruit, then appeared the tares also. So the servants of the householder came and said unto him, Sir, didst not thou sow good seed in thy field? from whence then hath it tares? He said unto them, An enemy hath done this. The servants said unto him, Wilt thou then that we go and gather them up? But he said, Nay; lest while ye gather up the tares, ye root up also the wheat with them. Let both grow together until the harvest: and in the time of harvest I will say to the reapers, Gather ye together first the tares, and bind them in bundles to burn them: but gather the wheat into my barn" (Matthew 13:24-30).

Matthew 13:24-30 was used by the Lord to illustrate the revelation that He had given me. The Lord said that you may be sowing good seeds (reading the Word, praying, going to church, helping the brotherhood) but there was a time while you were 'sleeping' or inactive in the things of the Lord (in your childhood or life in the world) when the enemy sowed weeds among your wheat or good seeds. For some of us, our time of 'sleep' are in those times when you are walking in disobedience to the will of God, and have not acknowledged nor accepted Jesus Christ as your Lord and Savior. For most of us, that time of 'sleep' is in our childhood (a time filled with concerns other than God).

The Lord continued to explain how both the weeds and wheat grew and just as the servants asked, so too the people in your life may have asked, "Didn't you sow good seeds?" The answer was yes! I did, but I had unresolved hurts and pains growing too.

Where then did these weeds come from? He answered with the use of a memory. "It came from a time when you were a child and you had looked for things and did not receive it." For me, it did not take much for a seed to be planted and burst out with roots. I did not have certain things in my life such as a Christian upbringing, an outlet to speak what was in my heart, and a mentor to teach me how to cope or overcome. Furthermore, my family had deep rooted issues, all suitable conditions for the enemy's seed to germinate. Understand that it is important that as a parent you provide the right conditions for your children. And if you are a pastor or a part of the body of Christ, it is paramount that you provide the right conditions for God's people according to His Word.

Christian Upbringing:

"Train up a child in the way he should go: and when he is old, he will not depart from it" (Proverbs 22:6).

Counselor:

"There is that speaketh like the piercings of a sword: but the tongue of the wise is health" (Proverbs 12:18).

"Without counsel purposes are disappointed: but in the multitude of counsellors they are established" (Proverbs 15:22).

Mentor:

"Remember them which have the rule over you, who have spoken unto you the word of God: whose faith follow, considering the end of their conversation" (Hebrews 13:7).

"The aged women likewise, that they be in behavior as becometh holiness, not false accusers, not given to much wine, teachers of good things; That they may teach the young women to be sober, to love their husbands, to love their children, To be discreet, chaste, keepers at home, good, obedient to their own husbands, that the word of God be not blasphemed" (Titus 2:3-5).

"Iron sharpeneth iron; so a man sharpeneth the countenance of his friend" (Proverbs 27:17).

Family issues:

"The fathers shall not be put to death for the children, neither shall the children be put to death for the fathers: every man shall be put to death for his own sin" (Deuteronomy 24:16).

"And, ye fathers, provoke not your children to wrath: but bring them up in the nurture and admonition of the Lord" (Ephesians 6:4).

"Fathers, provoke not your children to anger, lest they be discouraged" (Colossians 3:21).

The Lord identified my time of 'sleep' and as fast as He showed me the events, I remembered the negative emotions that were attached to them. He also explained how what the enemy was trying to do was to have me do and think the opposite of what God requires. For example, there were times when I was a child where I felt I was taken advantage of. The result of this, left me feeling that I was no longer going to be anyone's doormat. Here, the enemy's plan was to destroy the gift of serving God and others. God's plan is for us to serve but the enemies' plan is for us to be selfish.

The next thing to happen in Matthew chapter 13 was that the servants asked to uproot the weeds. The Lord then said that He has been allowing both seeds to grow for a while in my own life so that I could identify the weeds from the wheat. There were times when the weeds tried to stifle the wheat. Hence, the reason why sometimes we may pray and ask God to remove or keep us from committing a sin only to see them resurface, sometimes overshadowing the good that is within us. He further said that He was ready for His work to be completed in me and it was now harvest time. Just as the owner of the field had to wait to see the weeds among the wheat before uprooting them, so did I. During the wait, the Lord brought me to a place where I was ready to accept that I had a tree rooted in negative feelings. Most of which were rooted in unforgiveness, a major stronghold that you will read about later. I was now prepared and equipped with the Word of God to uproot the tree of the enemy and have the Lord's roots deeply grounded and rooted within me. The Lord then gave me the same instruction as identified in the Matthew 13:30. I was to collect the weeds, burn them and gather the wheat into the barn.

The following were the steps given to me and that one should also follow under the guidance of the Holy Spirit to set one's heart free:

Step 1: Draw the tree of the enemy and identify all its roots that were planted in your heart.

Step 2: Draw the tree of God to replace the tree of the enemy. (For example, where hate was a root, I had to put love as the root.)

Step 3: Uproot it with the use of prayers, faith and confession of the Word of God with your mouth.

Step 4: Plant the tree of God within your heart [or store your good wheat in your barn] using prayers, faith and word confession according to the Word of God. Continually confess the Word of God until it is made manifest.

Step 5: Resist the enemy for he will try to attack and if you fall into temptation, be quick to repent so that it does not take root.

CHAPTER II

A Study of the Heart

"He fashioneth their hearts alike;
he considereth all their works"
(Psalm 33:15).

At this point, I would like to expound on the importance of our hearts toward [or unto] God, for it is the place from which He controls, instructs, tests and communicates with us.

"And thou shalt remember all the way which the LORD thy God led thee these forty years in the wilderness, to humble thee, and to prove thee, to know what was in thine heart, whether thou wouldest keep his commandments, or no" (Deuteronomy 8:2).

"But, O LORD of hosts, that judgest righteously, that triest the reins and the heart, let me see thy vengeance on them: for unto thee have I revealed my cause" (Jeremiah 11:20).

"And the LORD hardened the heart of Pharaoh, and he hearkened not unto them; as the LORD had spoken unto Moses" (Exodus 9:12).

"In the first year of Cyrus king of Persia, in order to fulfill the word of the Lord spoken by Jeremiah, the Lord moved the heart of Cyrus king of Persia to make a proclamation throughout his realm and also to put it in writing:" (Ezra 1:1 NIV).

"But thanks be to God, which put the same earnest care into the heart of Titus for you" (2 Corinthians 8:16).

"But Sihon king of Heshbon would not let us pass by him: for the LORD thy God hardened his spirit, and made his heart obstinate, that he might deliver him into thy hand, as appeareth this day" (Deuteronomy 2:30).

"O LORD, why hast thou made us to err from thy ways, and hardened our heart from thy fear? Return for thy servants' sake, the tribes of thine inheritance" (Isaiah 63:17).

"But the LORD said unto Samuel, Look not on his countenance, or on the height of his stature; because I have refused him: for the LORD seeth not as man seeth; for man looketh on the outward appearance, but the LORD looketh on the heart" (1 Samuel 16:7).

"For the word of God is quick, and powerful, and sharper than any two-edged sword, piercing even to the dividing asunder of soul and spirit, and of the joints and marrow, and is a discerner of the thoughts and intents of the heart" (Hebrews 4:12).

Do you know that God has a heart of His own?

"And I will give you pastors according to mine heart, which shall feed you with knowledge and understanding" (Jeremiah 3:15).

"And when he had removed him, he raised up unto them David to be their king; to whom also he gave their testimony, and said, I have found David the son of Jesse, a man after mine own heart, which shall fulfil all my will" (Acts 13:22).

"And it repented the LORD that he had made man on the earth, and it grieved him at his heart" (Genesis 6:6).

"And the LORD smelled a sweet savor; and the LORD said in his heart, I will not again curse the ground any more for man's sake; for the imagination of man's heart is evil from his youth; neither will I again smite any more everything living, as I have done" (Genesis 8:21).

God designed our hearts to be the gateway to our souls, the house of light, and His storage warehouse, so that we can be rooted in the love of Christ. I pray that after reading the following, you will give God full ownership of your heart.

"That he would grant you, according to the riches of his glory, to be strengthened with might by his Spirit in the inner man; That Christ may dwell in your hearts by faith; that ye, being rooted and grounded in love, May be able to comprehend with all saints what is the breadth, and length, and depth, and height; And to know the love of Christ, which passeth knowledge, that ye might be filled with all the fulness of God" (Ephesians 3:16-19).

Here we learn that Christ wants to make His home in our hearts, but there is a condition. The condition is that you trust in Him. You must trust that He will justify you if you were wronged, forgive you if you have sinned, replace your hurts and pains with joy and happiness, and turn your weaknesses into strengths. Trust Him and put all your hopes in Him. Please note that we cannot and will not be able to trust Him if we do not uproot the tree of the enemy. Leaving the tree of the enemy and doing nothing about it is like saying "I don't want God handling my problems." This means that you are not ready to let go. Ephesians 3 goes on to say what He promises if we trust Him. He will not only make His home in our heart but that our roots will grow deep down into God's love and keep us strong in Him. There is no going back unless you want to. He also wants us to have power to understand how wide, how long, how high, and how deep is His love. There are no surface roots with God, but they are roots that go deeper than the deepest ocean.

Trusting God with all our heart is the condition to unlocking ALL of God's promises.

"Let us go right into the presence of God with sincere hearts fully trusting him. For our guilty consciences have been sprinkled with Christ's blood to make us clean, and our bodies have been washed with pure water. Let us hold tightly without wavering to the hope we affirm, for God can be trusted to keep his promise" (Hebrews 10:22-23 NLT).

"The LORD is my strength and my shield; my heart trusted in him, and I am helped: therefore, my heart greatly rejoiceth; and with my song will I praise him" (Psalm 28:7).

"Trust in the LORD with all thine heart; and lean not unto thine own understanding" (Proverbs 3:5).

Some other conditions of our heart that God requires are:

o   *It must love:*

> *"Jesus said unto him, Thou shalt love the Lord thy God with all thy heart, and with all thy soul, and with all thy mind"* (Matthew 22:37).

o   *It must be tender and compassionate:*

> *"And be ye kind one to another, tenderhearted, forgiving one another, even as God for Christ's sake hath forgiven you"* (Ephesians 4:32).

o   *It must be at peace:*

> *"And let the peace of God rule in your hearts, to the which also ye are called in one body; and be ye thankful"* (Colossians 3:15).

> *"And the peace of God, which passeth all understanding, shall keep your hearts and minds through Christ Jesus"* (Philippians 4:7).

> *"I am leaving you with a gift—peace of mind and heart. And the peace I give is a gift the world cannot give. So don't be troubled or afraid"* (John 14:27 NLT).

o   *It must be filled with light:*

"For God, who commanded the light to shine out of darkness, hath shined in our hearts, to give the light of the knowledge of the glory of God in the face of Jesus Christ" (2 Corinthians 4:6).

"I pray that your hearts will be flooded with light so that you can understand the confident hope he has given to those he called—his holy people who are his rich and glorious inheritance" (Ephesians 1:18 NLT).

o *It must be believing and have faith:*

"That if thou shalt confess with thy mouth the Lord Jesus, and shalt believe in thine heart that God hath raised him from the dead, thou shalt be saved. For with the heart man believeth unto righteousness; and with the mouth confession is made unto salvation" (Romans 10:9-10).

o *It must be meek and humble:*

"Take my yoke upon you, and learn of me; for I am meek and lowly in heart: and ye shall find rest unto your souls" (Matthew 11:29).

o *It must be cheerful:*

"A merry heart doeth good like a medicine: but a broken spirit drieth the bones" (Proverbs 17:22).

o *It must be carefree and not troubled:*

"And take heed to yourselves, lest at any time your hearts be overcharged with surfeiting, and drunkenness, and cares of this life, and so that day come upon you unawares" (Luke 21:34).

"Let not your heart be troubled: ye believe in God, believe also in me" (John 14:1).

o *It must be near God:*

"Wherefore the Lord said, Forasmuch as this people draw near me with their mouth, and with their lips do honor me, but have removed their heart far from me, and their fear toward me is taught by the precept of men" (Isaiah 29:13).

o *It must be broken:*

"The LORD is nigh unto them that are of a broken heart; and saveth such as be of a contrite spirit" (Psalm 34:18).

"The sacrifices of God are a broken spirit: a broken and a contrite heart, O God, thou wilt not despise" (Psalm 51:17).

o *It must be cleansed and pure:*

"Let us draw near with a true heart in full assurance of faith, having our hearts sprinkled from an evil

conscience, and our bodies washed with pure water" (Hebrews 10:22).

"Truly God is good to Israel, even to such as are of a clean heart" (Psalm 73:1).

"Blessed are the pure in heart: for they shall see God" (Matthew 5:8).

"Who can say, I have made my heart clean, I am pure from my sin?" (Proverbs 20:9).

○ *It must be moved by God:*

"Then the family heads of Judah and Benjamin, and the priests and Levites—everyone whose heart God had moved—prepared to go up and build the house of the Lord in Jerusalem" (Ezra 1:5 NIV).

○ *It must be set on seeking God:*

"And ye shall seek me, and find me, when ye shall search for me with all your heart" (Jeremiah 29:13).

"And he did evil, because he prepared not his heart to seek the LORD" (2 Chronicles 12:14).

○ *It must not regard sin:*

"If I regard iniquity in my heart, the Lord will not hear me:" (Psalm 66:18).

o *It must be understanding and discerning:*

"Give therefore thy servant an understanding heart to judge thy people, that I may discern between good and bad: for who is able to judge this thy so great a people?" (1 Kings 3:9).

o *It must be poured out before the Lord:*

"Arise, cry out in the night: in the beginning of the watches pour out thine heart like water before the face of the LORD: lift up thy hands toward him for the life of thy young children, that faint for hunger in the top of every street" (Lamentations 2:19).

o *It must be upright and with integrity:*

"Do good, O Lord, unto those that be good, and to them that are upright in their hearts" (Psalm 125:4).

"Thou hast neither part nor lot in this matter: for thy heart is not right in the sight of God" (Acts 8:21).

"My defense is of God, which saveth the upright in heart" (Psalm 7:10).

"And if thou wilt walk before me, as David thy father walked, in integrity of heart, and in uprightness, to do according to all that I have commanded thee, and wilt keep my statutes and my judgments" (1 Kings 9:4).

o   *It must rejoice in the Lord:*

"And they of Ephraim shall be like a mighty man, and their heart shall rejoice as through wine: yea, their children shall see it, and be glad; their heart shall rejoice in the LORD" (Zechariah 10:7).

o   *It must be and remain true to the Lord:*

"When he arrived and saw what the grace of God had done, he was glad and encouraged them all to remain true to the Lord with all their hearts" (Acts 11:23 NIV).

o   *It must be perfect with the Lord:*

"Let your heart therefore be perfect with the LORD our God, to walk in his statutes, and to keep his commandments, as at this day" (1 Kings 8:61).

o   *It must be prayerful:*

"Now Hannah, she spake in her heart; only her lips moved, but her voice was not heard: therefore Eli thought she had been drunken" (1 Samuel 1:13).

"And before I had done speaking in mine heart, behold, Rebekah came forth with her pitcher on her shoulder; and she went down unto the well, and drew water: and I said unto her, Let me drink, I pray thee" (Genesis 24:45).

o *It must be set right with God:*

> **"And might not be as their fathers, a stubborn and rebellious generation; a generation that set not their heart aright, and whose spirit was not stedfast with God"** (Psalm 78:8).

> **"For their heart was not right with him, neither were they stedfast in his covenant"** (Psalm 78:37).

Understand that your heart is a storehouse. It can be a storehouse of God or of the devil.

"Bind them upon thy fingers, write them upon the table of thine heart" (Proverbs 7:3).

"But what saith it? The word is nigh thee, even in thy mouth, and in thy heart: that is, the word of faith, which we preach;" (Romans 10:8).

"Then I said, I will not make mention of him, nor speak any more in his name. But his word was in mine heart as a burning fire shut up in my bones, and I was weary with forbearing, and I could not stay" (Jeremiah 20:9).

"And all the kings of the earth sought the presence of Solomon, to hear his wisdom, that God had put in his heart" (2 Chronicles 9:23).

"And these things hast thou hid in thine heart: I know that this is with thee" (Job 10:13).

"Thy word have I hid in mine heart, that I might not sin against thee" (Psalm 119:11).

"Even as it is meet for me to think this of you all, because I have you in my heart; in as much as both in my bonds, and in the defense and confirmation of the gospel, ye all are partakers of my grace" (Philippians 1:7).

"And thus are the secrets of his heart made manifest; and so falling down on his face he will worship God, and report that God is in you of a truth" (1 Corinthians 14:25).

"But Mary kept all these things, and pondered them in her heart" (Luke 2:19).

"And these words, which I command thee this day, shall be in thine heart:" (Deuteronomy 6:6).

"This is an evil among all things that are done under the sun, that there is one event unto all: yea, also the heart of the sons of men is full of evil, and madness is in their heart while they live, and after that they go to the dead" (Ecclesiastes 9:3).

"For from within, out of the heart of men, proceed evil thoughts, adulteries, fornications, murders, Thefts, covetousness, wickedness, deceit, lasciviousness, an evil eye, blasphemy, pride, foolishness" (Mark 7:21-22).

"But Peter said, Ananias, why hath Satan filled thine heart to lie to the Holy Ghost, and to keep back part of the price of the land?" (Acts 5:3).

Good and evil cannot dwell in the same place, hence the reason why God separated the light from darkness. He never designed it for the two to dwell together.

"And God saw the light, that it was good: and God divided the light from the darkness" (Genesis 1:4).

If we have love in our hearts then there will be no hate, and if we have hate in our hearts then there will be no love. Having just identified the many benefits of our heart being the home of Christ, we are now going to look at the heart as the home of the devil and the great deal of destruction it produces.

"For from within, out of the heart of men, proceed evil thoughts, adulteries, fornications, murders, Thefts, covetousness, wickedness, deceit, lasciviousness, an evil eye, blasphemy, pride, foolishness" (Mark 7:21-22).

"For out of the heart proceed evil thoughts, murders, adulteries, fornications, thefts, false witness, blasphemies:" (Matthew 15:19).

You may say that man in general will have these within their hearts, but I want to take you to Luke 6:45 to show you that a man only brings out what is inside of him.

"A good man out of the good treasure of his heart bringeth forth that which is good; and an evil man out of the evil treasure of his heart bringeth forth that which is evil: for of the abundance of the heart his mouth speaketh" (Luke 6:45).

You should be convinced now more than ever to have the heart of Christ and to remove the tree of the enemy planted within it. However, if you are still not convinced I pray that the following scripture verse will convince you.

"For this people's heart is waxed gross, and their ears are dull of hearing, and their eyes they have closed; lest at any time they should see with their eyes and hear with their ears, and should understand with their heart, and should be converted, and I should heal them" (Matthew 13:15).

Now ask yourself this question, who and what should your heart reflect? We have life with Christ and death with the devil.

"As in water face answereth to face, so the heart of man to man" (Proverbs 27:19).

The Word of God describes how everything begins, happens and is stored in the heart.

The good that happens in the heart:

o   *Accepting others:*

"O ye Corinthians, our mouth is open unto you, our heart is enlarged" (2 Corinthians 6:11).

o   *Application/ instruction:*

"Bow down thine ear, and hear the words of the wise, and apply thine heart unto my knowledge" (Proverbs 22:17).

"Apply thine heart unto instruction, and thine ears to the words of knowledge" (Proverbs 23:12).

"So, teach us to number our days, that we may apply our hearts unto wisdom" (Psalm 90:12).

"So that thou incline thine ear unto wisdom, and apply thine heart to understanding;" (Proverbs 2:2).

o *Belief:*

"That if thou shalt confess with thy mouth the Lord Jesus, and shalt believe in thine heart that God hath raised him from the dead, thou shalt be saved. For with the heart man believeth unto righteousness; and with the mouth confession is made unto salvation" (Romans 10:9-10).

o *Changes:*

"How shall I give thee up, Ephraim? how shall I deliver thee, Israel? how shall I make thee as Admah? how shall I set thee as Zeboim? mine heart is turned within me, my repentings are kindled together" (Hosea 11:8).

o *Comfort:*

"That their hearts might be comforted, being knit together in love, and unto all riches of the full assurance of understanding, to the acknowledgement of the mystery of God, and of the Father, and of Christ;" (Colossians 2:2).

o *Decision to give:*

"Every man according as he purposeth in his heart, so let him give; not grudgingly, or of necessity: for God loveth a cheerful giver" (2 Corinthians 9:7).

o *Deep fervent love:*

"Seeing ye have purified your souls in obeying the truth through the Spirit unto unfeigned love of the brethren, see that ye love one another with a pure heart fervently" (1 Peter 1:22).

o *Desires:*

"Delight thyself also in the LORD: and he shall give thee the desires of thine heart" (Psalm 37:4).

o *Faithfulness:*

"And foundest his heart faithful before thee, and madest a covenant with him to give the land of the Canaanites, the Hittites, the Amorites, and the Perizzites, and the Jebusites, and the Girgashites, to give it, I say, to his seed, and hast performed thy words; for thou art righteous:" (Nehemiah 9:8).

o *Forgiveness:*

"So likewise shall my heavenly Father do also unto you, if ye from your hearts forgive not every one his brother their trespasses" (Matthew 18:35).

o *Gladness:*

"And on the three and twentieth day of the seventh month he sent the people away into their tents, glad and merry in heart for the goodness that the LORD had shewed unto David, and to Solomon, and to Israel his people" (2 Chronicles 7:10).

o *Knowledge of God's correction:*

"Thou shalt also consider in thine heart, that, as a man chasteneth his son, so the LORD thy God chasteneth thee" (Deuteronomy 8:5).

o *Obedience:*

"But God be thanked, that ye were the servants of sin, but ye have obeyed from the heart that form of doctrine which was delivered you" (Romans 6:17).

o *Parent-child relationship:*

"And he shall turn the heart of the fathers to the children, and the heart of the children to their fathers, lest I come and smite the earth with a curse" (Malachi 4:6).

o *Perfection:*

"But the high places were not taken away out of Israel: nevertheless, the heart of Asa was perfect all his days" (2 Chronicles 15:17).

o *Plans:*

   "A man's heart deviseth his way: but the LORD directeth his steps" (Proverbs 16:9).

   "There are many devices in a man's heart; nevertheless, the counsel of the LORD, that shall stand" (Proverbs 19:21).

o *Pleasing meditation:*

   "Let the words of my mouth, and the meditation of my heart, be acceptable in thy sight, O LORD, my strength, and my redeemer" (Psalm 19:14).

o *Praise:*

   "I will praise thee with my whole heart: before the gods will I sing praise unto thee" (Psalm 138:1).

o *Purity:*

   "Blessed are the pure in heart: for they shall see God" (Matthew 5:8).

o *Rejoices:*

   "Thy words were found, and I did eat them; and thy word was unto me the joy and rejoicing of mine heart: for I am called by thy name, O LORD God of hosts" (Jeremiah 15:16).

"Therefore, did my heart rejoice, and my tongue was glad; moreover, also my flesh shall rest in hope" (Acts 2:26).

"And Hannah prayed, and said, My heart rejoiceth in the LORD, mine horn is exalted in the LORD: my mouth is enlarged over mine enemies; because I rejoice in thy salvation" (1 Samuel 2:1).

o   *Remembering the works of God:*

"Only take heed to thyself, and keep thy soul diligently, lest thou forget the things which thine eyes have seen, and lest they depart from thy heart all the days of thy life: but teach them thy sons, and thy sons' sons;" (Deuteronomy 4:9).

o   *Security:*

"His heart is established, he shall not be afraid, until he see his desire upon his enemies" (Psalm 112:8).

o   *Sing and make music:*

"Speaking to yourselves in psalms and hymns and spiritual songs, singing and making melody in your heart to the Lord;" (Ephesians 5:19).

o   *Soundness:*

"A sound heart is the life of the flesh: but envy the rottenness of the bones" (Proverbs 14:30).

o *Trust:*

   ***"Trust in the LORD with all thine heart; and lean not
   unto thine own understanding"*** (Proverbs 3:5).

   ***"The LORD is my strength and my shield; my heart
   trusted in him, and I am helped: therefore, my heart
   greatly rejoiceth; and with my song will I praise him"***
   (Psalm 28:7).

o *Truth:*

   ***"He that walketh uprightly, and worketh
   righteousness, and speaketh the truth in his
   heart"*** (Psalm 15:2).

o *Understanding:*

   ***"Make the heart of this people fat, and make their
   ears heavy, and shut their eyes; lest they see with
   their eyes, and hear with their ears, and
   understand with their heart, and convert, and be
   healed"*** (Isaiah 6:10).

o *Unity:*

   ***"And they, continuing daily with one accord in the
   temple, and breaking bread from house to house, did
   eat their meat with gladness and singleness of heart"***
   (Acts 2:46).

○ *Willingness:*

"Then Hezekiah answered and said, Now ye have consecrated yourselves unto the LORD, come near and bring sacrifices and thank offerings into the house of the LORD. And the congregation brought in sacrifices and thank offerings; and as many as were of a free heart burnt offerings" (2 Chronicles 29:31).

○ *Wisdom:*

"The wise in heart shall be called prudent: and the sweetness of the lips increaseth learning" (Proverbs 16:21).

"When wisdom entereth into thine heart, and knowledge is pleasant unto thy soul;" (Proverbs 2:10).

"Wisdom resteth in the heart of him that hath understanding: but that which is in the midst of fools is made known" (Proverbs 14:33).

"And all the earth sought to Solomon, to hear his wisdom, which God had put in his heart" (1 Kings 10:24).

○ *Work ethic:*

"So we rebuilt the wall till all of it reached half its height, for the people worked with all their heart" (Nehemiah 4:6 NIV).

"And whatsoever ye do, do it heartily, as to the Lord, and not unto men;" (Colossians 3:23).

The evil that happens in the heart:

o *Abominations:*

"When he speaketh fair, believe him not: for there are seven abominations in his heart" (Proverbs 26:25).

o *Adultery:*

"But I say unto you, That whosoever looketh on a woman to lust after her hath committed adultery with her already in his heart" (Matthew 5:28).

"And they that escape of you shall remember me among the nations whither they shall be carried captives, because I am broken with their whorish heart, which hath departed from me, and with their eyes, which go a whoring after their idols: and they shall loathe themselves for the evils which they have committed in all their abominations" (Ezekiel 6:9).

o *Anguish:*

"For out of much affliction and anguish of heart I wrote unto you with many tears; not that ye should be grieved, but that ye might know the love which I have more abundantly unto you" (2 Corinthians 2:4).

o *Astray:*

"Wherefore I was grieved with that generation, and said, They do alway err in their heart; and they have not known my ways" (Hebrews 3:10).

o *Being against others:*

"For as he thinketh in his heart, so is he: Eat and drink, saith he to thee; but his heart is not with thee" (Proverbs 23:7).

o *Corruption:*

"He that hath a froward heart findeth no good: and he that hath a perverse tongue falleth into mischief" (Proverbs 17:20).

o *Crying:*

"And they have not cried unto me with their heart, when they howled upon their beds: they assemble themselves for corn and wine, and they rebel against me" (Hosea 7:14).

o *Deceit:*

"The heart is deceitful above all things, and desperately wicked: who can know it?" (Jeremiah 17:9).

"Frowardness is in his heart, he deviseth mischief continually; he soweth discord" (Proverbs 6:14).

o *Despise correction:*

   "And say, How have I hated instruction, and my heart despised reproof;" (Proverbs 5:12).

o *Discouragement:*

   "Whither shall we go up? our brethren have discouraged our heart, saying, The people is greater and taller than we; the cities are great and walled up to heaven; and moreover, we have seen the sons of the Anakims there" (Deuteronomy 1:28).

o *Distress:*

   "Behold, O LORD; for I am in distress: my bowels are troubled; mine heart is turned within me; for I have grievously rebelled: abroad the sword bereaveth, at home there is as death" (Lamentations 1:20).

o *Doubt:*

   "For verily I say unto you, That whosoever shall say unto this mountain, Be thou removed, and be thou cast into the sea; and shall not doubt in his heart, but shall believe that those things which he saith shall come to pass; he shall have whatsoever he saith" (Mark 11:23).

o *Enticed/seduction:*

   "If mine heart have been deceived by a woman, or if I have laid wait at my neighbour's door;" (Job 31:9).

o *Envy:*

"Let not thine heart envy sinners: but be thou in the fear of the LORD all the day long" (Proverbs 23:17).

o *Foolish/ fools:*

"Because that, when they knew God, they glorified him not as God, neither were thankful; but became vain in their imaginations, and their foolish heart was darkened" (Romans 1:21).

"Foolishness is bound in the heart of a child; but the rod of correction shall drive it far from him" (Proverbs 22:15).

"The fool hath said in his heart, There is no God. They are corrupt, they have done abominable works, there is none that doeth good" (Psalm 14:1).

o *Giving grudgingly:*

"Thou shalt surely give him, and thine heart shall not be grieved when thou givest unto him: because that for this thing the LORD thy God shall bless thee in all thy works, and in all that thou puttest thine hand unto" (Deuteronomy 15:10).

o *Greed:*

"And they come unto thee as the people cometh, and they sit before thee as my people, and they hear thy

words, but they will not do them: for with their mouth they shew much love, but their heart goeth after their covetousness" (Ezekiel 33:31).

o *Grief:*

"Then said Elkanah her husband to her, Hannah, why weepest thou? and why eatest thou not? and why is thy heart grieved? am not I better to thee than ten sons?" (1 Samuel 1:8).

"Thus my heart was grieved, and I was pricked in my reins" (Psalm 73:21).

o *Hardness:*

"Happy is the man that feareth alway: but he that hardeneth his heart shall fall into mischief" (Proverbs 28:14).

o *Hastiness:*

"Be not rash with thy mouth, and let not thine heart be hasty to utter anything before God: for God is in heaven, and thou upon earth: therefore, let thy words be few" (Ecclesiastes 5:2).

o *Hatred/ despised:*

"Thou shalt not hate thy brother in thine heart: thou shalt in any wise rebuke thy neighbor, and not suffer sin upon him" (Leviticus 19:17).

"And it came to pass, as the ark of the covenant of the LORD came to the city of David, that Michal, the daughter of Saul looking out at a window saw king David dancing and playing: and she despised him in her heart" (1 Chronicles 15:29).

○ *Haughtiness:*

"But when his heart was lifted up, and his mind hardened in pride, he was deposed from his kingly throne, and they took his glory from him:" (Daniel 5:20).

○ *Iniquity:*

"And if he come to see me, he speaketh vanity: his heart gathereth iniquity to itself; when he goeth abroad, he telleth it" (Psalm 41:6).

○ *Lies:*

"In transgressing and lying against the LORD, and departing away from our God, speaking oppression and revolt, conceiving and uttering from the heart words of falsehood" (Isaiah 59:13).

○ *Lust:*

"Lust not after her beauty in thine heart; neither let her take thee with her eyelids" (Proverbs 6:25).

"And it shall be unto you for a fringe, that ye may look upon it, and remember all the commandments of the LORD, and do them; and that ye seek not after your own heart and your own eyes, after which ye use to go a whoring:" (Numbers 15: 39).

o *Madness:*

"This is an evil among all things that are done under the sun, that there is one event unto all: yea, also the heart of the sons of men is full of evil, and madness is in their heart while they live, and after that they go to the dead" (Ecclesiastes 9:3).

o *Own imagination:*

"But have walked after the imagination of their own heart, and after Baalim, which their fathers taught them:" (Jeremiah 9:14).

o *Perverseness:*

"They that are of a froward heart are abomination to the Lord: but such as are upright in their way are his delight" (Proverbs 11:20).

o *Pride:*

"The pride of thine heart hath deceived thee, thou that dwellest in the clefts of the rock, whose habitation is high; that saith in his heart, Who shall bring me down to the ground?" (Obadiah 1:3).

o *Remembering past evil:*

   "For oftentimes also thine own heart knoweth that thou thyself likewise hast cursed others" (Ecclesiastes 7:22).

o *Schemes to do wrong/ wickedness:*

   "Because sentence against an evil work is not executed speedily, therefore the heart of the sons of men is fully set in them to do evil" (Ecclesiastes 8:11).

   "For their heart studieth destruction, and their lips talk of mischief" (Proverbs 24:2).

   "Yea, in heart ye work wickedness; ye weigh the violence of your hands in the earth" (Psalm 58:2).

o *Sorrow/ heaviness:*

   "Therefore, remove sorrow from thy heart, and put away evil from thy flesh: for childhood and youth are vanity" (Ecclesiastes 11:10).

   "Wherefore the king said unto me, Why is thy countenance sad, seeing thou art not sick? this is nothing else but sorrow of heart. Then I was very sore afraid" (Nehemiah 2:2).

   "Heaviness in the heart of man maketh it stoop: but a good word maketh it glad" (Proverbs 12:25).

"A merry heart maketh a cheerful countenance: but by sorrow of the heart the spirit is broken" (Proverbs 15:13)

"That I have great heaviness and continual sorrow in my heart" (Romans 9:2).

o   *Thoughts of evil:*

"Repent therefore of this thy wickedness, and pray God, if perhaps the thought of thine heart may be forgiven thee" (Acts 8:22).

"For from within, out of the heart of men, proceed evil thoughts, adulteries, fornications, murders," (Mark 7:21).

o   *Unbelief:*

"Take heed, brethren, lest there be in any of you an evil heart of unbelief, in departing from the living God" (Hebrews 3:12).

o   *Unrepentant:*

"But after thy hardness and impenitent heart treasurest up unto thyself wrath against the day of wrath and revelation of the righteous judgment of God;" (Romans 2:5).

o   *Unrighteous utterance:*

"But those things which proceed out of the mouth come forth from the heart; and they defile the man" (Matthew 15:18).

o *Wrath:*

"But the hypocrites in heart heap up wrath: they cry not when he bindeth them" (Job 36:13).

It can then be concluded that everything happens in the heart or are the result of the condition of our hearts.

"For where your treasure is, there will your heart be also" (Matthew 6:21).

CHAPTER III

Guard Your Heart

"Above all else, guard your heart,
for it is the wellspring of life"
(Proverbs 4:23 NIV).

Be careful after uprooting the tree of the enemy that you guard your heart always, for it is the wellspring of life, the new and fulfilled life in Christ. Remember, the aim of the enemy is to get us built up with emotional baggage and negative feelings in our hearts towards God, self and others.

Matthew 12:43-45 says, "When the unclean spirit is gone out of a man, he walketh through dry places, seeking rest, and findeth none. Then he saith, I will return into my house from whence I came out; and when he is come, he findeth it empty, swept, and garnished. Then goeth he, and taketh with himself seven other spirits more wicked than himself, and they enter in and dwell there: and the last state of that man is worse than the first. Even so shall it be also unto this wicked generation."

One very important condition that the Lord wants me to expound on is that of the emptying and filling of the heart as mentioned earlier. We all know that when a person leaves a house or a building it becomes empty or is left unoccupied. Well, it is the same with the heart. When the tree of the enemy is uprooted, the heart will be left empty. However, God does not want it to be kept empty but to be filled with His love and light. For it is clearly seen in Matthew 12:43-45 above, that when an evil spirit comes out of a man and returns to the house that it left and finds it empty, swept clean and put in order, it goes and take with it seven other spirits back into the house. This reading goes on to say that the man's final condition will become worse than the first. In other words, if after completing the uprooting process and you do not fill your heart with the roots or tree of Christ and His Word, then the enemy can plant his tree there once more, worse than the first. Remember, first empty, then fill.

"My son, give me thine heart, and let thine eyes observe my ways" (Proverbs 23:26).

"And ye shall seek me, and find me, when ye shall search for me with all your heart" (Jeremiah 29:13)

"My eyes will watch over them for their good, and I will bring them back to this land. I will build them up and not tear them down; I will plant them and not uproot them. I will give them a heart to know me, that I am the LORD. They will be my people, and I will be their God, for they will return to me with all their heart" (Jeremiah 24:6-7 NIV).

"Yea, I will rejoice over them to do them good, and I will plant them in this land assuredly with my whole heart and with my whole soul" (Jeremiah 32:41).

During my encounter with the Lord, He instructed me to write and share this revelation with His people that they may be set free, in order that His purpose for their lives would be fulfilled without any hindrances. It is because of these trees being present in our hearts that we sin and give the enemy legal grounds to torment us.

CHAPTER IV

Strongholds

"For the weapons of our warfare are not carnal,
but mighty through God to the pulling
down of strong holds;"
(2 Corinthians 10:4).

While identifying the main roots and the negative symptoms associated with the tree of the enemy, they are the four major strongholds that open us up to being demon oppressed or possessed: Unforgiveness, Rejection, Rebellion, and Bitterness.

The major root, the foundation of these four, is unforgiveness. In life one may be rejected and even rebel as a result of rejection. However, if we do not forgive those who rejected us, or hurt us in some way, including those who we rebelled against, or even if we do not forgive ourselves, then we give the enemy legal grounds – that is legal grounds to make us bitter. In the story of the woman who was caught in the act of adultery, we can see that she had rebelled against the Word of God that says one shall not commit adultery. In addition to her rebellion, she was now rejected by men. However, the one who was most important amongst all men,

44 | upROOTED

Jesus Christ, did not reject nor condemn her. Instead He forgives and admonishes her to go and not continue in her rebellion against God.

"And they which heard it, being convicted by their own conscience, went out one by one, beginning at the eldest, even unto the last: and Jesus was left alone, and the woman standing in the midst. When Jesus had lifted up himself, and saw none but the woman, he said unto her, Woman, where are those thine accusers? hath no man condemned thee? She said, No man, Lord. And Jesus said unto her, Neither do I condemn thee: go, and sin no more" (John 8:9-11).

The story that depicts the greatest act of forgiveness was that of Jesus on the cross. Jesus was horribly rejected my men. Though He was scorned, mocked, bruised and beaten He did what His Father would want him to do. And that was to ask for the forgiveness of man.

"Then said Jesus, Father, forgive them; for they know not what they do. And they parted his raiment, and cast lots" (Luke 23:34).

One of the most important aspects of a Christian life is forgiveness as seen in the bible verses that follow about forgiveness of self and others and receiving forgiveness from God. 1 John 1:9 shows that if we repent and ask forgiveness He will forgive us and purify us from all unrighteous. As you can see forgiveness comes before purification from all unrighteousness including rejection, rebellion and bitterness.

So too in Acts 2:38 we see that after forgiveness we receive the gift of the Holy Spirit.

"If we confess our sins, he is faithful and just to forgive us our sins, and to cleanse us from all unrighteousness" (1 John 1:9).

"Then Peter said unto them, Repent, and be baptized every one of you in the name of Jesus Christ for the remission of sins, and ye shall receive the gift of the Holy Ghost" (Acts 2:38).

To not give the enemy legal grounds means to ask forgiveness for our own sinful thoughts, words and deeds and those of others. In other words, if your mother rejected you from birth, ask the Lord to forgive her and you also forgive her. Do not harbor the ill feelings of the rejection in your heart. If you have rebelled against God's will for your life, quickly ask forgiveness, and forgive yourself and live according to the Word of God. As you forgive others, so too the Lord forgives you.

"For if ye forgive men their trespasses, your heavenly Father will also forgive you: But if ye forgive not men their trespasses, neither will your Father forgive your trespasses" (Matthew 6:14-15).

These four strongholds, Unforgiveness, Rejection, Rebellion and Bitterness are the sources from which all issues arise. They are the main roots that give birth to all other problem roots. Today, I urge you to begin the process, asking for the guidance of the Holy Spirit, to receive your healing and deliverance. The harvest is here, it's now time to set your heart free!

CHAPTER V

Setting Your Heart Free

*"If the Son therefore shall make you free,
ye shall be free indeed"
(John 8:36).*

INSTRUCTIONS:

○ Read and highlight the negative symptoms listed below that you have been experiencing. You may notice that you have highlighted more symptoms under a particular stronghold; this just means it is the main root affecting your heart, or the title of the tree planted.

○ When you are identifying the things you feel and experience, the Holy Spirit may bring you back to events (memories) in your life where you felt the emotions. Be sure to keep a note of them. This is to ensure that you address them.

○ After searching your heart complete the five steps that follow to receive your deliverance.

Unforgiveness

UNFORGIVENESS: The three **types of unforgiveness are for self, God and others.** Unforgiveness is the cause of many health problems, and struggles in life. It can be defined as not pardoning the sins that you have committed and/or others have committed against you.

Feelings associated with Unforgiveness: anger, hate, rage, disgust, sadness, unpeaceful, unclean, victimized, resentment, and hurt.

Examples of times when persons may choose not to forgive:

- After being abused (especially sexually).
- Giving up your virginity unwillingly.
- Inheritance is given to others and not you.
- When a spouse cheats.
- Sudden death of a loved one.
- If born with a disability.
- When someone has wronged you.
- When someone has offended you.

Symptoms of Unforgiveness: For others

o When you think of the person who has wronged you, feelings of hate and unhappiness arise.

- You have no desire to have anything to do with the person who has wronged you.
- Avoid the person at all cost.
- You cannot find one good thing to say about the person.
- When you speak about the event you get choked up and cannot continue.
- Every time you think of the time you were wronged you get emotional, either angry or emotional; you cry a lot.
- You constantly recite speeches of what you are going to say to them, or what you should have said to them.
- You think that they should hurt as much as you were hurt or pay for what they have done to you.
- You think of ways or plan how to get back at them.
- When you see the person, you are overwhelmed with emotions.
- You cannot pray for the person.
- Get angry when they accomplish something.
- You do not wish to talk or have the person in your presence.
- Cannot look at the person.
- Do not make yourself available to help the person.
- Have a hard time admitting when you are wrong.
- Always make accusations against the person.

- You complain a lot about the person.
- You tell lies or alter stories about the person.
- You create stories about the person because you do not want others to speak or get close to the person but instead be on your side.
- Blame the person for the hurt and pain that you have and for your life being the way it is.
- It is very easy for you to have evil thoughts about the person.
- Constantly bring up past hurts which continue to remain fresh in your mind no matter how much time has passed.
- You don't want them to touch, hug or kiss you.
- If it is your spouse, you don't want him or her to lay down with you.
- Make them feel guilty to make you feel good.
- Have a lack of compassion or hate for the person.
- Believe that the person is the one with the problem and/or is influenced by demons.
- When the person makes a mistake, you remind them of all the other mistakes that they have made. You keep a list of all their wrongs.
- You do not want to forget the things that they would have done so, you constantly recite it or right them down.

- Your love for others may be fading.
- You have mood swings and always have a 'foul' attitude.
- Other: _____

Symptoms of Unforgiveness for yourself:

- Feel disappointed with yourself.
- Feel that you can never do anything good or right.
- Feel worthless and hopeless.
- Neglect care of yourself.
- Find it hard receiving gifts or compliments, believing that you don't deserve it.
- Feel ashamed of what you would have done.
- Feel guilty and need to be repaid for your wrong.
- Spend time trying to make up or fix things.
- Wish that you would have never done what you did.
- Think 'how could I be so stupid'.
- Feel that you deserve bad treatment.
- Feel that God does not want to hear from you and so this causes you not to pray and/or ask Him for anything.
- Think that God is mad with you and every time something bad happens, believes that he is punishing you.

o Believe that you don't deserve to be happy.

o Feels that your prayer is not answered because of your sin.

o Other: _____

Symptoms of Unforgiveness for God:

o Blame God for not stopping or allowing the things to happen.

o Do not believe in His Word; especially where He speaks well of us (e.g. we are His treasured possession) and speaks concerning the situation.

o Think, "If God loved me then why He would make this happen to me?"

o You would rather struggle with the situation than give it to God.

o Refuse to bear the fruits of the spirit (love, joy, peace...)

o Other: _____

Calculate how many symptoms you believe you are exhibiting and write it below.

Total: _____

Rejection

REJECTION: There are two types of Rejection: rejection from others and self-rejection.

Rejection can begin as early as in the womb as in the case of unplanned/ unwanted pregnancies.

Emotions/feelings associated with rejection: Do you feel any of the following? Abandoned, denied, discarded, inadequate, cast-off, isolated, neglected, deserted, refused, excluded, or useless.

Examples of rejection:

- A parent to a child, "I did not want you, you were a mistake."
- Having been asked to leave a home.
- Getting high grades in school, behaving well and still not acknowledged for it.
- Loving someone who does not love you back.
- Being treated as an outcast among your other siblings.
- Wanting to meet your estranged dad or mom only to know he does not want to meet you.
- Being abused or abandoned by parents.
- Struggle with identity issues such as not knowing who you really are and what you bring to the world. Also

relying on parents or other authority figures for their approval as to who you are.

- Your opinion or voice is not heard. Always being told to "shut up'.
- Other: _____

Symptoms of rejection: Put a tick (check) in the ones you experience.

o Made-up or pretend qualities: pretending to be somebody you aren't, just to be accepted or to hide your real self.

o Do not approach persons or speak up because of fear of being rejected.

o Fear of telling someone how you feel, anticipating rejection.

o Most of the time rejecting others, even at first instance.

o Believing the lie that no one will stay in your life no matter what they say or how good they are to you.

o Always questioning whether a person rejects or accepts you.

o Trying to please everyone so that they will accept you and tell you something good about yourself. Wanting others to consider you as important.

o Victim mentality- feeling bad for yourself as in "Poor me" or this only happens to me attitude.

- Feeling that everyone is taking advantage of you, that they only want to use you.
- Do not like to be corrected or criticized. Any suggested correction always leaves you feeling like you are a failure or not good enough.
- Feelings of being unloved and all alone.
- Feelings of "I don't belong" or "I'm not wanted."
- Blame God, thinking that He made it happen, or thinking it is because He made me this way.
- Act the opposite of being withdrawn to overcompensate, and instead acting arrogant when rejected.
- Insecure about yourself and others.
- Head-strong personality. Believing you are always right about things and know everything as a way of protecting yourself from being rejected.
- Always look for approval or acceptance for things you do.
- Feel jealousy or anger towards others, especially if things seem to be going well for them.
- Feels jealous when a loved one gives their time to others.
- Needs or desires all the attention.
- Avoids confrontation because of fear of being told about your faults or weaknesses.
- Feelings of "I already feel bad about myself, I don't need anyone else to tell me."

o Harboring feelings that nobody wants me, or nobody cares about me.

o Feelings of insignificance and as if you are a waste of space and anyone else's time.

o Feelings of having no purpose. Asking why God can't just take me out of the world?

o Express a 'clingy' behavior.

o Feels that whatever I have to say is not important, so I am not going to say it.

o Always starting a sentence and then stopping and saying, "It's ok, forget about it, it does not matter."

o Feel that if the people who are supposed to love me don't, then how can a stranger or anyone else?

o Feel like you have been taken advantaged of or even used as a slave or servant.

o Have a doormat mentality, allowing others to walk over you.

o Have an anti-doormat mentality, as a bully.

Other: _____

Calculate how many symptoms you believe you are exhibiting and write the total below.

Total: _____

Rebellion

REBELLION can be defined as being disobedient, self-willed, defiant, stubborn, and oppositional. Rebellion comes from not wanting to submit or having a desire to have one's way with disregard for others.

Emotions/feelings associated with rebellion: Resisting, revolt and disregard for others.

Examples of Rebellion:

- A husband takes breakfast at 8 a.m. but because he forgot to kiss his wife goodnight, she instead makes no breakfast.
- A child was told that he cannot go to a dance competition that he really wanted to attend because he did not do his chores, however he went out and came back late.
- An educated wife refuses to take any advice or follow instructions from her uneducated husband simply because he is not on the same level as her.
- A brother serving in a church for 5 years was passed over for a position as usher for another brother who entered the church a year ago. The first brother now refuses to do anything for the leaders and other members of the church.

Symptoms of Rebellion:

o   Feel that persons (such as parents) have ruled me all my life, now it is time that I have control.

o   Feel a need to take care of myself, and look out for myself because no one else will.

o   Feel that I am going to do everything that pleases me, despite what others think.

o   When angry with someone, ignore that person's wishes, like or dislikes.

o   Question or object every time directions or instructions are given.

o   When silenced by someone, feel like "Who do they think they are talking to?" and continue to talk anyway.

o   Have a hard time conforming to the rules of a group. Ignore rules or regulations.

o   Read the Word of God but refuse to do some or most of the things that God requires (you pick and choose only what you want to do).

o   Have a hard time being a doer of the Word of God.

o   Do not care what others have to say or reject the opinion of others.

o   Seem to enjoy and start conflicts.

o Feel that your own dreams or desires were pushed aside and, so you try to ensure that you are no longer tossed aside.

o Seek dominance in all things.

o Disregard the beliefs or lifestyle of others.

o Feel that you don't have to receive consent or approval from others, e.g. spouse.

o Feel like you don't care about anything or anyone.

o Do not care for the needs or desires of others.

o Do not regret the hurts and pain you may have caused others.

o Feel that someone is always trying to take control from you.

o Other: _____

Calculate how many symptoms you believe you are exhibiting and write it below.

Total: _____

Bitterness

BITTERNESS can be defined as spiritual or emotional poison. It comes from having unwanted experiences, goals unaccomplished, letdowns, and/or hindrances in life (rejection, rebellion, unforgiveness and failures). It develops when one chooses not to or finds it hard to let go of hurts and pains. Bitterness is connected with Unforgiveness.

Feelings associated with bitterness: anger, hatred, resentment, retaliation, depression, cranky, discontented, sorrowful, never satisfied, regret, and selfish.

Examples of things that can lead to bitterness:

- All examples identified under unforgiveness, rejection and rebellion.
- Not getting married.
- Not being able to own a house.
- Not being able to bear children.
- Not finishing school, or not going to college.
- Not landing your dream job.
- Marriage not lasting.
- Expectations you have for yourself are not being fulfilled.

Symptoms of Bitterness:

Most of the ones already identified under unforgiveness, rejection and rebellion.

FAILURES OR UNACCOMPLISHED EXPECTATIONS:

- Feel like a failure and can't seem to do anything right.
- Feel that maybe you did not deserve what happened to you.
- Always talk about the things that you could have done or wanted to do.
- Feel saddened or get depressed when thinking of the things not accomplished.
- Always make statements like "I could have been making a lot of money now."
- Keep things that remind you of an unaccomplished expectation or dream.
- Get very angry when someone has the opportunity to do what you were not able to do.
- Live your dreams vicariously in others.
- Desire or insist that your children do the things that you wanted to do even though they don't want to.
- Stop dreaming or desiring life to be an expected way.
- Have no plans for the future.

o   Feel like it makes no sense praying for it thinking that you wouldn't get it anyway.

o   Thinking that you have failed or will fail at everything.

o   Put down the dreams of others, especially your own children/ discourage them from dreaming.

o   Tries to control and manipulate others.

o   Always expect the worst.

o   Exhibit a fear of failure.

o   Doubt yourself.

o   Seem unable to learn from your mistakes.

o   Do not want to be reminded of past failures, get angry or depressed when thinking of it.

o   Always negative, see the negative in everyone and everything.

o   Other: _____

Calculate how many symptoms you believe you are exhibiting and write it below.

Total: _____

CHAPTER VI

The Root of the Matter

*"Looking diligently lest any man fail of the grace
of God; lest any root of bitterness springing up
trouble you, and thereby many be defiled;"*
(Hebrews 12:15)

STEP ONE: Draw and label the tree of the enemy planted within your heart, identifying all its roots and/or symptoms as highlighted under the strongholds.

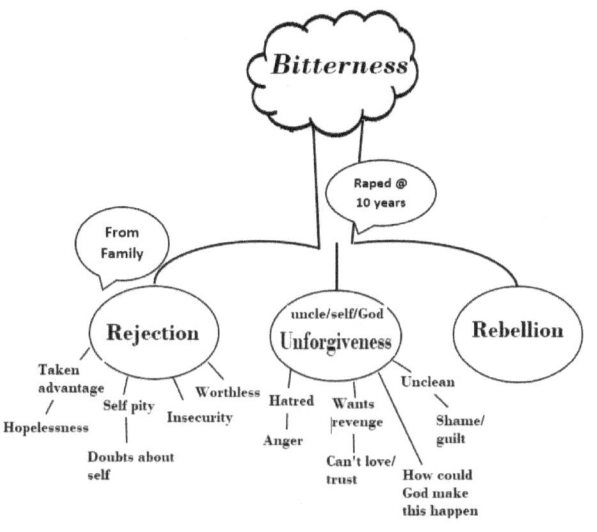

"For if the firstfruit be holy, the lump is also holy:
and if the root be holy, so are the
branches" (Romans 11:16).

STEP TWO: Draw the tree of God to replace the tree of the enemy. (For example, where hate was a root, put love as the root).

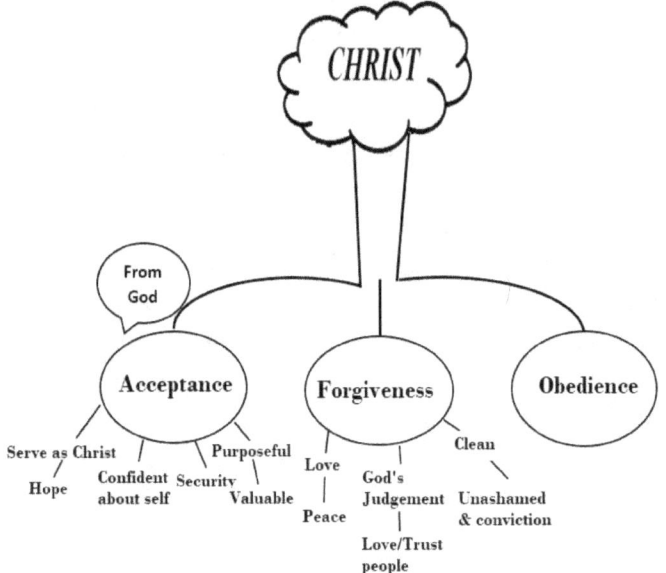

"... Gather ye together first the tares, and bind
them in bundles to burn them ..."
(2 Kings 19:30).

STEP THREE: Uproot and destroy each root with the use of prayers, faith and confession of the Word of God with your mouth.   Remember to call the name of each root and renounce it.

Example: Heavenly Father,

I repent of my sins. Forgive me Lord for not committing my hurts, pains and past experiences unto you so that you may bring peace to my heart. Forgive me for harboring them in my heart and allowing them to take root. Wherever I would have brought it upon myself knowingly or unknowingly, I ask for your forgiveness. I forgive myself and all those who have wronged me. I pray that the root of rejection along with all its other roots such as being taken advantage of, hopelessness, self-pity, insecurity, doubts about myself and self-worthlessness be uprooted right now by your great and mighty power, in the name of Jesus. I renounce you, spirit of rejection. I bind and cast you, with all of your roots and demons, out of my heart and back into the deepest pit of hell where you belong. That's where you are meant to be rooted, not in my heart. Not in the heart that God has given me. You do not belong there, you have no residence there. I serve you an eviction notice; depart from within my heart... (Prayer continued in Step 4).

> *"And the remnant that is escaped of the house of Judah shall yet again take root downward, and bear fruit upward. For out of Jerusalem shall go forth a remnant, and they that escape out of mount Zion: the zeal of the Lord of hosts shall do this"*
> *(2 Kings 19:30-31).*

STEP FOUR: Plant the tree of God within your heart (barn) using prayers and word confession according to the Word of God.

…I declare that you, <u>root of rejection,</u> along with all your roots have been removed and you are replaced with the root of Christ. I now speak <u>the root of acceptance and all the other roots associated with it the root of hope, to serve as Christ, confidence about myself in security, value, and a purposeful life, to be</u> deeply rooted, into my heart. Lord, I welcome you to take up residence in my heart because that is where you belong. I thank you for delivering and healing my heart from rejection and I pray that every empty space in my heart be filled with the light of Christ by the power of the name of Jesus.

Continually (everyday) confess the Word of God until it is made manifest in your life. Pray the Word of God concerning your issues. (Example: being taken advantage of). Father, you're calling for us to serve you and others as Christ served. Your Word says in Luke 6:27-28 & 30 ***"But I say unto you which hear, Love your enemies, do good to them which hate you, Bless them that curse you, and pray for them which despitefully use you… Give to every man that asketh of thee; and of him that taketh away thy goods ask them not again."*** I pray that your word will be made manifest in my life. I pray that I may be a living example of your word.

Your Word says in Mark 10:44-45 ***"And whosoever of you will be the chiefest, shall be servant of all. For even the Son of man came not to be ministered unto, but to minister, and*** *to give his life a ransom for many."* And I pray that I will be a servant of the Lord just as Christ was.

"Be sober, be vigilant; because your adversary the devil, as a roaring lion, walketh about, seeking whom he may devour:"
(1 Peter 5:8).

STEP FIVE: Resist the enemy for he will try to attack you and if you fall into temptation be quick to repent in order that it does not take root.

When thoughts come you can rebuke it and send it back to the devil, think on the things of Christ and/or speak the Word of God against it. Remember to resist the enemy and he shall flee.

James 4:7- *"Submit yourselves therefore to God. Resist the devil, and he will flee from you."* If or when the temptation/devil comes you can instantly resist him. Then you know that your deliverance is sure. However, if you find it difficult to resist, then you need to go back to the drawing board. Maybe you had some resistance in denouncing or some unforgiveness, or that your faith has wavered.

Remember, you do not want to empty your hearts and leave it empty because the devil will come back and plant a tree that is going to be much worse than the first one. Please ensure that your heart is filled with the light and love of Christ. Until you begin to think, act or speak the way God wants you to keep reading His Word concerning your situation.

Deliverance is not a one- time event but a continuous process. Keep praying the Word of God concerning every issue. Speak those things that are not as though they were: Romans 4:17- *"(As it is written, I have made thee a father of many nations,) before him whom he believed, even God, who quickeneth the dead, and calleth those things which be not as though they were."*

Always examine your heart hereafter to know if you are in right standing with the Lord. 1 John 3:19-22 says *"And hereby we know that we are of the truth, and shall assure our hearts before him. For if our heart condemn us, God is greater than our heart, and knoweth all things. Beloved, if our heart condemn us not, then have we confidence toward God. And whatsoever we ask, we receive of him, because we keep his commandments, and do those things that are pleasing in his sight."* If you are in right standing your heart will not condemn you but if you are not, it will. This should be an indicator of the status of your heart.

Conclusion

This may be the end of the book but it's the beginning of a bountiful life for you in God with your now cleansed and renewed heart, mind and soul. I find it paramount to make known the origin of the title of my book, "upROOTED." When I was given the name for the book the Lord asked specifically that the word 'up' be written lowercase and the word 'rooted' in uppercase. He said that the most important thing to Him is that we be rooted in Him. Hence, the reason for the word rooted being in uppercase. For us to be rooted we must uproot the trees planted by the enemy. What you have done here today has pleased the Lord and has opened up for you a greater and deeper communion with Him. John 8:11 records what Jesus said to the woman who was caught in adultery, "*... **And Jesus said unto her, Neither do I condemn thee: go, and sin no more,**"* and as Christ has said I urge you to maintain a heart free of the enemy but filled with God. Amen.

About the Author

NADINA WILLIAMS

Nadina Williams has never settled for the status quo. The fourth child of a sea captain and homemaker, she was born on the small island of Carriacou, Grenada. She always loved reading books and writing stories and poems, but never did she believe she would write a book one day and become a published author.

In 2005, at the young age of seventeen, she left her small island to attend college on another small island—Manhattan, otherwise known as New York City. While there, she found the Lord and has since dedicated her life to His will by serving in youth ministry, worship ministry, intercessory prayer, and deliverance ministry. At the end of her stay in the Big Apple, she had earned her bachelor of professional studies in human services from Metropolitan College of New York in 2008.

The Lord instructed her to return home to work with the youth. Two exciting events happened as a result of her obedience: she met her soon-to-be husband. Secondly, she got a position as a guidance counselor at one of the only two high schools on her island: Bishop's College. She loved working with teenagers, knowing the Lord had truly given her the grace and compassion for helping them and taking on the role of youth advocate. She also assists her husband with his track and field club, and she and her husband make a formidable team in building and rebuilding the lives of the young people.

Believing the students deserved the best, Williams wanted to expand her knowledge and skills. So, after six years at Bishop's College, she received a scholarship to pursue her masters in psychological science at the University of North Florida in Jacksonville, Florida, with a graduation date of April 2018.

Nadina enjoys her hectic schedule, solely dedicating her time to God, family, and work.

www.ingramcontent.com/pod-product-compliance
Lightning Source LLC
Chambersburg PA
CBHW071537080526
44588CB00011B/1695